This book is dedicated
to everybody who has
second-guessed themselves.

———

*Remember… instincts
are everything.*

THE UNQUALIFIED HOSTESS

WHOOPI

The
Unqualified
Hostess

RIZZOLI
NEW YORK

GOLDBERG

CONTENTS

INTRODUCTION

Yes, that's my name on the cover—it *is* Whoopi Goldberg, it's not a mistake! What you're holding in your hands is a book I put together because I figured that if you're like I was, you probably believe that you don't have any taste. But I'm here to tell you that you do! I hope that if you look through the book you will be pleasantly surprised, and you might learn a thing or two. I'll show you what *I've* learned about how to set a table that makes any occasion—whether it's a noisy family holiday, an afternoon tea party, or a casual dinner with a few friends—feel special and unique.

Now, you won't be able to do everything the way I do it, but you can do everything I do the way *you* do it. And who's gonna tell you that's wrong? If they try, don't listen to them. Shock 'em! Instead of feeling bad—feel great! 'Cause you looked at this book and you thought, "Well, if *Whoopi* can do this, so can I." Do you know how to make it feel like you're having a great adventure at *your* table? No … because you've forgotten how to have a good time! That's what this book is for. I'm going to help you find a way to have a good time for yourself. One would think that I do a lot of this for my grandkids or my great-granddaughter—it's not, it's for me! Because I like having fun at the table. It takes time, but it's worth it.

Here is the other thing that this book will do for you, and you have to be prepared for it because it's annoying: it's going to slow you down. But trust me, that's a good thing! It's going to make you go through the things you have and actually think

I'm going to help you find a way to have a good time for yourself!

Let yourself break the "rules"

about them. Where did this one come from? Where did I buy it, or who gave it to me? A lot of it has meaning, or a memory attached, and that's all part of the fun. Some of those memories will make their way to your table, if you want them to.

You'll notice that there are a few things I repeat throughout this book, and one of them is: I have a LOT of stuff! I want you to be prepared for what you see because it *looks* like I'm a hoarder . . . but I'm not. I'm just someone who had a great opportunity to collect things I was interested in. And sometimes I'd collect things that I didn't know anything about, which made me want to learn more about them and then they so surprised me that I just collected more! This book is not just about what is physically on your table; it's also about giving yourself permission to have fun. So I believe that's what everyone should have: excess.

When I was a little girl, my mother expected the table to be set every day for breakfast, lunch, and dinner. So we all took turns: me, my mother, and my brother, Clyde. Each place setting would have a plate, a glass, a fork, a knife, and a spoon (sometimes two spoons if we were having soup and dessert or tea). In those days, we washed everything (and I mean *everything*, from underwear to pedal-pushers!) by hand in our tiny bathroom sink, and we hung it to dry over the tub. We didn't have much, but my mother taught us to take good care of the things we had.

If you're lucky enough to have a home, you're ahead of the game, because many people don't feel like they have one. I have a home. It's where I live, it's where my stuff is; it's where my smell is. I happen to spend a lot of time here, because when I go out, I go out as "Whoopi," which can be a lot of work. So whether I'm throwing a big holiday party or just sitting down for a dinner alone, I want my home to be a place where I *want* to be: stimulating and fun. That's home for me. And I think that if you're lucky enough to have a home, you should show it some love. Set the table, even if it's just you. Throw some petals into the mix—flowers make everything better. Let yourself break the "rules"; if there's a toy that would make you smile, put it on the table. It doesn't cost a lot of money to do what we're doing here, because this is all about the stuff you already have, and how to celebrate it.

There's already enough darkness in the world— so I'm all for cheer. This book is kind of like a little beacon of light, one that signals: "Hey! There's some fun over here!" 'Cause I love anything that makes me smile, and I figure if it makes me smile, it might make you smile. Flip the page—I think you'll have a good time!

DINNER PARTY

This is probably the "straightest" table you will find in this book, but don't worry:

Something odd will eventually show up!

This is a different kind of vibe; this table's really about the plates, and I chose this for our first table because they're the reason I started to throw dinner parties.

I was in New Orleans, and wanted to check out a place called M.S. Rau's, because I had been getting their catalogue for years, and loved their stuff. I spotted these plates, and as you can see, they appear to have Ws on them, and I learned they were from the King of Hanover's set. I saw that M.S. Rau had one hundred and twenty of these place settings (which includes the plate, the bowl, the salad plate, etc.). So I asked the seller, "Could I just buy . . . twelve of them?" And they said okay! Always ask 'cause you never know!

So once I had these King of Hanover plates, with the W (and the little crown on top!), I thought to myself: "Well . . . I guess I should probably invite some people over to eat!"

I haven't used them in ages, but I wanted to open the book with them because they're my first and oldest high-end plates, and they started a whole new tradition for me.

Let's start here.

You're looking at this saying, "Well, I don't have all
this stuff! You said I would be able to do what you do—
you lie, woman!" I do not lie… knowingly. Everything that
you see here exists in your kitchen: you have dishes, you
have glasses, you have silverware, you have a tablecloth.
All this is exactly what you're looking at
—— *so do not panic.* ——

I'm going to show you how I
lay out a table, as it was shown to me
by very, very heady people.

Flip the page…

These look coordinated because they are coordinated. But yours don't have to be. You can have any kind of layout you want. I have my way, and there are some traditional ways, but you decide how you want your table to be.

———

There are some basics: you have to use a fork (unless you're eating sushi), you have to use a spoon, you have to use a knife. Now, I've included a lot of other stuff here, because I could. But when you're laying a table, the first thing you want to think about is:

What's the order of the meal?
What are you eating first?

SALAD FORK

SOUP SPOON

BUTTER KNIFE

DINNER KNIFE

DINNER FORK

TABLESPOON

DESSERT FORK

Some people like ice cream forks,
I do! Not everyone has them, but I'm a fan.

Historically speaking, napkins are
fairly new—no one really used napkins
even at the turn of the century.
Some rich people had napkins but
anyone else who was eating was wiping
their mouth on the tablecloth.

DESSERT SPOON

TEASPOON

Basically, this is it, you have this in your drawer—go ahead and open it, I'll wait.

Each place setting gets the entrée plate on the bottom, the soup bowl on top of that, and a salad plate on top.

OK, I can feel you panicking—*do not panic!* Whatever bowl you have that you put soup in normally, you're gonna put it on the table. You're going to put it on top of your dinner plate. Yeah, it's more to wash up later on, but that's another conversation for later in the book.

Typically, I position each of the plates so that they're facing the same direction—I want my guests to see the same thing when they each sit down. Things just have to face the right way for me, or I get nervous! I'll walk around, making little adjustments. It's all open seating in my house, it feels too stuffy to arrange seating in advance.

The King of Hanover wouldn't have salad plates!

They didn't really do that in the 1800s—but I use these, which are kind of fun. Look closely: they're dogs! So I don't mind mixing them in. These go on top, because the salad is the first course you'll eat.

I'm a big
fan of knife rests.

———

They keep your tablecloth clean!
Knife rest, clean table.
Clean table? Happy host.

For serving wine

A glass with a big bowl is generally for red, smaller bowl is for white wine. If you have people who don't drink, give them another glass, *something cute!*

You have water glasses,
you have white wine glasses, and
you have red wine glasses. If you don't
have a whole lot of glasses, just use one!
Because this is your dinner party.

**If you want to use Welch's
grape juice glasses or Flintstones
glasses, do that.**

But you have the option of using
all kinds of sizes if you
have them.

Yes, these are salt and pepper shakers—the smallest ones you've ever seen. If you have more than three people to dinner, it can be annoying to wait for someone to pass the salt, so you may want to have another pair of shakers in your house. As for the ones you see here, you'd be hard-pressed to find them because these are one of the most unusual things in my collection. And I've never been able to find them again.

Since the first thing you're going to have is your salad, the salad fork is the furthest fork to your left.

Next you'll have soup, so the spoon is the middle.

Then comes the main course, so that larger dinner fork will be the third one, closest to your plate.

THIS IS MY LAYOUT; OTHERS MAY DO IT DIFFERENTLY. (IF YOU DO SOUP THAT'S COLD, START WITH THAT.)

I like white napkins—you don't have to...

I know it looks like the petals are a little excessive— they are, much like myself—but flowers are everything.

This is also a look you can do without spending —— a lot of dough. ——

Head down to the store, bodega, or the 7-Eleven—wherever you see they are selling flowers—and ask the person how long those flowers have been sitting there (the ones that say $1.99). Wait until you can say to them, "Can I buy those from you for fifty cents?" Take them home, trim the stems, and let them sit in some warm water. Then you rub 'em and spin 'em, until the heads pop off and the petals come apart easily. So for less than a buck, if you're a good negotiator, you now have created a table people say they can't do.

Look at your chairs, measure them out, and see what size they are.... And then?

Get yourself some chair covers.

I'm telling you, they are the best investment. The covers are maybe $4.99.
This way when kids and guests spill on them, you won't lose your mind. It doesn't
matter how much your chairs cost when you bought 'em, you'll want to keep 'em
looking good! If you don't like the plain cover by itself, you can wrap a ribbon
around it, or get out your glue gun and tie a bow.

Whenever you have crystal or glass for your wine, you always want to run your pinky around the rim and make sure there are no nicks in it–don't want anybody to cut their lip. And the guests won't know that we put our fingers on the rim ('til they read the book).

On the back of some of these plates, you'll spot some porcelain staples; this is how they put broken porcelain back together. The man at M.S. Rau was telling me about the porcelain staples when I found this set. So I said to give me a lot of the stapled ones, because

I don't want *perfection* on the table; I want a *story*.

I mean, who knew there were porcelain staples?

I was at a friend's house, and as she set her table, I noticed her pile of plates looked a little weird. Turned out, she had put a felt circle in between each plate, and she explained to me that it kept the plates from breaking and scratching each other, because we stack them up without realizing the weight of them.

OK, kids, did you figure out what the "something odd" was?

—

It's the little people literally hanging out all over the place.

So, four people show up at your house,
and they look hungry—maybe they've driven
or even walked a very long distance:

Now, you are obligated, according to the big book of friendship, to feed them!

That is what this lunch table is laid out for.... But only if four of them show up—if eight of them show up, maybe you order pizza (but keep the table looking good). Food is not as important here, when your friends just come by to hang with you.

So I always try to make the table look fun, and as you can see this is more of a table design for the women I know, as opposed to a mixed crowd. (Men's shoes on wine glasses just don't look as nice!) I even ran out of my kitchen and grabbed some flowers and cut them from my garden.*

Now, what you see here is my everyday stuff—the things I use for me, or when my family comes over (because they do like to eat, and they like when I provide the food). Go into your closet and pull out some stuff. A bowl for soup, a salad plate, a regular plate for a sandwich. But no rule says you have to give people soup, or even a salad. Nothing says they even have to stay for more than a drink! But if you're feeling magnanimous, these are things you can do at your table.

*OK, that's a lie. Here's what I did: I took some jars and I put some flowers in them, because flowers (as I say all throughout this book) make a table come alive.

33

Sandwiches
— make —
life simple!

Somebody gave me these glasses, and I thought they were fun, so I put them on the table because who doesn't love a high heel wine glass?!

Lunch really only became a tradition during the 19th century when people started working longer and longer shifts at factories, which pushed dinner back to the evening. Those workers needed some kind of break for the middle of the day, and eventually they were given an hour off to eat what we now call lunch. Betcha didn't know that!

Big
mistake.

If you're going to serve people food at your house, here's the stuff you must pay attention to:

Are they allergic to peanuts, to fish? How about gluten? These are questions you really do have to ask, because there's nothing worse than someone's face blowing up five sizes because you didn't ask them, and they didn't tell you, that they don't eat shrimp! All you have to do is ask, *"Do you eat meat? Are you a vegetarian? A pescatarian? An Episcopalian?!"*

This silverware
pattern is "First Love,"
by Rogers Brothers.
It's just everyday silver,
but I think it looks
great, so Deco.

If you're wondering how all this stuff got here, well: there are really wonderful people out there who feel compelled to send me birthday presents, Christmas presents, house gifts, just things that they found that they thought I would like.

And I appreciate all of it … but it can be difficult to thank people, because sometimes I can't remember! And some of it's from family, like my mom and my brother.

A lot of the stuff that you see is stuff that has been with me for a long time and I like using these things because it reminds me that somebody thought of me.

If there's ever a
time to run wild with
the mix and match, it's
when you've got those
good friends coming
by for lunch!

DINNER

FOR

ONE

Joy Behar's lasagna

My Kindle

You've seen how I like to celebrate with friends and family, but occasionally, it's just me.

Even when it's just you, take the time to set a nice table!

You'll be glad you did it because at the end of the day, your table should always be about whatever makes you feel happy and special. It starts when you slow down a little and make the effort. Doesn't have to be fancy or expensive! Even something as simple as laying out your silverware and folding your napkin can make a world of difference. Because it's not always about what you're eating—it's also about taking a moment for yourself.

Now, here I am looking really content because I've got my Kindle, I've got my iced tea, and I'm eating Joy Behar's lasagna. There is something on the table that I would not touch with a twenty-five-foot pole, but people always say, "Well, just put it on the table, maybe you'll try it." So that's why there's kale on the table, and that kale is about fifteen years old. I don't promise you'll eat it, I don't promise you'll want to, but it may make you chuckle as you look at this thing you're never gonna eat.

Did you know that the first American restaurant to use a tablecloth was Delmonico's in downtown New York? Delmonico's was also the first place that a woman could sit by herself and eat a meal. If there was a woman on her own in Delmonico's, they did not let men come over and bother her. That's what made it such a great place!

WHOOP'S

AFTERNOON TEA

I know, I know: y'all are looking at this going, "What? Tea?" I'm here to say, "Yeah! Tea!"

Shocking as this sounds, tea is really good for the soul.

Just creating a time to sit down and get fancy. Because I don't know about you, but every couple of weeks, I need to get fancy. And the best way to do it is to create a table that makes me smile and laugh and use all the crap that is in my house—it's all on the table right now. This is a cacophony of my brain, with the added luxury of really good scones.

In America, we don't ritualize tea like the Brits do, it's something you mostly drink when you're sick—you pour the water over the bag and that's what you have! But when I first went to England, I didn't know there was an entire ritual. And it takes forever! You've got the scones, and the clotted cream, you have the jam—all of that stuff. And that's a big part of what this book is about: taking the time to slow down. Life moves really fast, and we don't appreciate it as much unless we take a minute to have some fun, or learn something new. Welcome to Whoop's Afternoon Tea!

*Now, if you go out to
a restaurant for afternoon tea,
the server might tell you:*

"Start at the bottom tier, and work your way up to the sweets."

3 · TOP LAYER

As for that top tier, you can have any kind of dessert you want: it's your tea! I love these graham cracker shells because you can fill them with anything—Cool Whip, jam, Nutella—this top tier is the sweet finale! Unless you want to break all the "rules" and start with it . . . since rules are made to be broken.

2 · MIDDLE LAYER

Now for the middle layer, it's all about the scones! You'll want to make sure you have your favorite jam (here we've got strawberry), and maybe some lemon curd as well as clotted cream. The clotted cream you'll have to buy! Brits may make it themselves, but we Americans haven't gotten the hang of it. If you're feeling adventurous though, we'll tell you how, just in case.

1 · BOTTOM LAYER

So you'll see here that my bottom layer is what looks like a bunch of sandwiches, but this doesn't have to be a lot of work! Whatever you're in the mood for—it could be PB&J, it could be tuna fish, you decide—make two full-sized sandwiches. If you feel like getting fancy, trim off those crusts before you cut the sandwich into strips. But seriously, you can create the look that we have here using only two sandwiches—just slice them into sections.

I like fruit tea, so there's an *overabundance* of fruit tea in my house.

But
I would *never* pick somebody else's tea.

Tea is very specific,
people know what they like.
It can depend on their attitude,
where they're at that day.
I bring everyone into
the kitchen, open the drawers,
and I let them choose what
they want to drink.

Wish I could remember what kind — of tea this is! — It looks like there are little white pebbles in it, but they're not—this is what real tea looks like when it's not hidden by a bag.

This strange thing that looks like a basket sitting inside your tea cup is for loose tea— when it's not in a tea bag. When you pour water on it, it drips through the tea and into your cup. And the little silver dish that you see on the table is for resting your strainer so it doesn't leak tea onto your very nice tablecloth!

TEA BREW HOW-TO:

JAPANESE BREWING METHOD

In Japan, a matcha tea ceremony isn't just about how you brew the tea, it's also about creating harmony and equilibrium for the host and guests.

Formal invitations are sent out beforehand, and when guests arrive, they are told that the tea is ready to receive them before they are seated.

The host might use about 3 scoops of matcha powder per guest, adding it all into a communal tea bowl, before adding the hot water and stirring until it becomes a thin blended mixture.

When the bowl is ready, the first guest rotates it and takes a sip before wiping the rim of the bowl and passing it along to the next guest, who repeats the movements until the bowl makes its way back to the host.

CHINESE BREWING METHOD

In a Chinese tea ceremony, oolong is the most commonly used tea type. But the water itself is also very important! Ensuring that the water is pure and clean is one of the ways the Chinese tea ceremony honors and pays tribute to nature.

Tools for the preparation are also of huge importance. Traditionally you will need a Yixing or porcelain teapot, a tea pitcher or cha hai, a brewing tray, a teaspoon, and a tea strainer (with however many cups your guests need).

The person who pours the tea into the teapot will often raise the kettle to shoulder height, which becomes a kind of performance.

Oolong can be steeped anywhere from 1–10 minutes, and the tea is transferred to the tea pitcher before it is served to guests.

BRITISH BREWING METHOD

The British prefer strong black teas—either tea bags or loose tea. If you like loose tea, you'll need a strainer to hold it in either your cup or teapot. One teaspoon per cup of tea is the safe bet, generally. But if you're brewing a pot of tea, an extra teaspoon can't hurt.

Never microwave your water. Aside from it ruining the ritual, it's also unsafe. Fill a kettle, either stovetop or electric, and boil the water.

Place your tea in the cup or teapot, and then add the boiling water. Allow the tea to steep for 3–4 minutes, and then remove the tea from the cup or teapot. And enjoy!

INDIAN BREWING METHOD

In India, all tea is called "chai" (but if you want the spiced kind, you probably mean "masala chai"). Since this type of tea is brewed in milk and water over a stovetop, it's always piping hot when served.

You'll want to gather milk, water, strong black tea (a teaspoon of loose leaves), a slice of fresh ginger root, a few cardamom pods (smashed beforehand), a small chunk of cinnamon stick, some fennel seeds, and sugar.

Using two parts water to one part milk, combine all ingredients except the tea leaves in a saucepan over medium heat and bring to a simmer, then add the tea leaves and reduce to low heat, steeping until you achieve a caramel color. Then drain and serve!

WHOOPI BREWING METHOD

Not everybody likes strong tea.
I don't so I steep mine a little less.

Here's what I do:
Get yourself a tea bag.
And dip and pull... dip and pull...
dip and pull... blow, sip...
Grab a cookie. Go to town!

This is about fun, it's not about perfection.

Matchy-matchy is not my thing. Who wants to look around the table and see nothing but the same thing?

If you have a lot of stuff—and as you know, I have a *lot* of stuff—sometimes it sounds like a great idea to put everything on the table, but somebody's got to clean all that up... and it's usually me. So, not everything in this cabinet always makes it to the table. Sometimes it's just a question of, how much stuff do I want to put away?

I don't actually *collect* — I just have — things that make me happy.

Take what you've already got at your house — *and* — *have a party!*

I like to mix
the expected with the
unexpected

when it comes to my afternoon tea!
Follow the rules if you want to,
— *or* —
break them if it means you'll
have more fun.

If you're gonna buy desserts, taste them before you get them. There's nothing worse than a dessert that's too sweet, and it's on everybody's face but no one wants to say it.

Most people have different plates in their lives.... I like to use two of these, two of those…

Did I mention how much I love knife rests?!

They're not on everybody's radar, and so they're usually a bargain on auction websites and at thrift stores.

Jared's Clotted Cream

Clotted cream is always best made with unpasteurized heavy cream, but you can use regular cream, too. You have to put it in an oven at low temperature, 200°F, for twelve hours in a glass pan, covered. And then it separates, so all that nice fat comes to the top, and you get sort of a nice caramelized butter on the top as well.

—Jared Sexton, Bluebird London NYC

But back to
the scones, which
is why we're all here.

———

Keep in mind: smaller is better!
If it's too gigantic, no one will ever
finish it. Give each one a healthy
schmear of your favorite
topping…

… and then,
like a little piglet,
stuff it into your
mouth!

HALLOWEEN

You may think, "This year, I don't feel like doing *anything* for Halloween." Here's what I suggest:

Get some candy and decorations just in case!

Because if you say to yourself, "You know what? I wish I had some Halloween stuff to put in the window" . . . it's better to have it and not want it then to want it and not have it. There are so many fun things anybody can do. People don't do 'em because they think, "Oh, it's not worth it," but it so is. For yourself! Humoring oneself is, to me, the most important thing in the world. Why do you care what other people think? We give up all of this power to people who don't know us, and we tell them that they're in charge. Hell no! Not me.

There is no reason at all why you can't take the things that exist in your house—things that you bought, things that people have given you, things that you live with every day—and put them on a table. There's nothing you can't put on your table, there's no wrong answer here. This is your house. What do you want on your spooky table?

65

When you look at the flowers, take a closer look at the vases:

That's cobweb crepe paper wrapped around the base.

It's versatile, since it comes in patterns to accompany any party theme. It's inexpensive, you can find it at any drugstore or online. And yet it's the kind of detail that shows your guests you went the extra mile for them.

When it comes to dry ice, be very careful. But if you can be safe with it—i.e., watch those kids!—it's so much fun. Find some crazy cups for the table, add a little dry ice, a splash of water, and really set the Halloween mood.

Flowers in a vase are fine. But flowers in a vase wrapped in
skeleton ribbon and topped with a nesting blackbird are *special!*

Balloons are very important! You can
customize them for any occasion, and they
really fill out the room. Now, I'm a lazy
woman—I'm not gonna lie. So I go to the
balloon boutique for mine, because I'm not
gonna blow 'em up. If you feel like you have
the lungs of doom, give it a shot—but you're
gonna have to blow up a lot of them, because
you want your party to look like *a party!*

———

I love using those wispy cobwebs because
they give that Halloween feel. Just be aware,
pulling them apart takes a lot longer than you
may think! Then of course you can put bugs on
them—I'm not a huge fan, but
some people like them.

I love toys, and they always find a place on every one of my Halloween tables—it's a great way to bring grand-parents and grandkids together.

There's nothing
real on this chandelier.

If you have lighting fixtures in your house, and
you can find a rim around them to attach things,
you can have a lot of fun during the seasons.
It doesn't have to be a big chandelier but it's
amazing what you can do with fake flowers and
fake leaves—every season you can change
your light fixtures, just wrap some
stuff around them!

It sounds crazy, but there's something great about coming out of your bedroom and looking over to see your light fixtures having a lil' fun.

I had a lot of
different stuff that I wanted
to play with on the chairs. I used all
this tulle I had lying around the house
(doesn't everybody have tulle lying
around the house?) but you can really
use anything to wrap a chair—crepe
paper, gauzy fabric, or tulle. Who's
going to tell you you didn't
do it right? *Nobody!*

I don't like wearing costumes.

—

But I *definitely* like throwing Halloween parties!

I try to throw Halloween parties for adults, but that rarely works out; there seem to be kids everywhere I go!

Rip out all of its inner guts
(it's kinda nasty so either enjoy it, or put on
some rubber gloves), then get a baking tray. Put a
little sea salt on it, and a little bit of cooking oil. Clean
off the pumpkin seeds, stick 'em on the tray, and bake them.

Take the cleaned-out pumpkin, cut it into pieces, and
bake face down. When it's soft enough, you can mash it up
for pumpkin pie recipes or whatever else you like.

If that's not your thing, I suggest you and your friends get all the
pumpkins together after Halloween, put them around the trunks
of trees, and let them become mulch, which feeds the tree.
I think it's important that after we use it, we send it back.

Of course you could carve it, but are you any good at that?
I've had too many pumpkins that look like family
members. Every time I carve one it ends up
looking like someone I know!

You'll see I have a real plate underneath the paper plate. People say to me all the time,

"Why do you do that?"

People always think that paper plates aren't elegant—they are, or can be, if you put 'em on top of something. You can do this trick with any theme: Christmas, Thanksgiving, birthdays.

I love fire when it's in a fireplace, but I'm not a big fan of candles. These are flameless candles, and they just … flicker! I love these because they look real, but they're battery operated, so no little kids are going to hurt themselves with this.

THANKSGIVING

I love the entire holiday season, I celebrate it all; but the truth of the matter is:

It all starts with Thanksgiving!

As a kid, you start a new school year, and then you're off and running from September straight to November. When you reach Thanksgiving, you know you've got it made: one long stretch of celebrations through to the New Year.

That whole span of time is something I recall even today—the house smelling like turkey meant the good times were starting. Everybody's feeling good, even during years when there was heavy stuff going on. When I was a kid, the Vietnam War was happening; but somehow the adults seemed to band together to make the holidays meaningful for us kids.

So for me, that's why I'm kind of obsessed with making fun tables and celebrating, because if we can't make ourselves feel happy and feel grateful, we run the risk of becoming some new kind of person, someone who allows social media to dictate who we are.

I happen to have a house with many rooms and a lot of space, and as you see from each of these chapters: I have a lot of stuff! But whatever is available in your house can and will make a beautiful table. It's all about imagination and creativity.

The theme of this table is: *What are you thankful for?*

So here's a picture of my brother, of my mom and me—actual pictures you can pick up. It's so important to take time to get photos printed—it's inexpensive and makes all the difference. We only take photos on our phone these days, because it's so convenient; but ironically, it makes the photos—the ones that we actually want to see and hold—less accessible to us. Physical photos help us never lose touch with the past.

Here's the thing about holiday food—someone's got to make it. If you're holding this book, it could be you. Now, I'm the one that makes the turkey for Christmas and Thanksgiving, because it's the only thing I know how to make! But that's okay.

Everybody does their part.

And listen, when you're making your turkey or whatever it is you're going to bring, just know that people are going to be grateful because they're eating for free. But if somebody says, "Well, this doesn't taste like my uncle's," just look at them and say, "This is free." That shuts them up.

When I was a kid,
my mom used to say to me:
"Nobody's named Emma anymore."

That was *her* name. And when she passed, I was cleaning
out her stuff, and I found two spoons, engraved with
"Emma."

My mom loved beautiful
things as well, and she taught me that beautiful
doesn't have to mean expensive. She found
buried treasure in every crazy little
store in her neighborhood.

Now, you don't
need a set of turkey plates
for Thanksgiving dinner;
but there's no better way to
show your guests you're not
messing around here.

I like
a separate
serving table
at Thanksgiving.

It allows folks to serve themselves more easily, and gives them the chance to talk to other people they might not be sitting with.

— But if you don't have the space —

the dishes sit right there on the table with you, and become part of your Thanksgiving spread!

You can find all kinds of stuff like this in stainless steel—doesn't have to be silver! A lot of the cutlery I use are pieces I bought on trips, and there's some Tiffany in the mix, too. But there are many less expensive options, including aluminum and electroplate (though like silver, you will have to polish it now and then).

Cranberry sauce...me, I like the canned stuff. I get that people make that fancy cranberry relish, but it's got too many things in it for me! **This? I don't know what's in it** and I'm happy. That's what I grew up with; it's simpler.

If the little kids are at the table with you, it can be fun to give them a slightly different place setting.

— *It's easier for them* —
and it's a chance to make
them feel special.

The age range
for this kind of table
is four to eight years old.

After eight, they can sit at the
big table, although you
should still "fun it up"
for them.

Have a little extra space in your dinner area? Make a separate table for the kids!

Cover it with a "tablecloth" that they can actually draw on, and not only will it keep them outta your hair, they'll also try to out-color each other and they won't pick up their phones.

You can make a kid's day with little more than a few bucks' worth of art supplies and a handful of the silliest stuff from the local party store.

TURKEY CAN TAKE A WHOLE NIGHT TO COOK, WHEN YOU DO IT MY WAY.
BUT IT'S WORTH IT — JUST MAKE SURE YOU HAVE A GOOD ALARM CLOCK!

Whoopi's Thanksgiving Turkey

ON THE NIGHT BEFORE THE BIG DAY...

1 — Get a butterball turkey, and about 9,000 sticks of butter.

2 — Preheat your oven to 280°F.

3 — Clean your turkey out, be sure to get those gizzards (sometimes they put two packages in there!).

4 — Make your stuffing — I like Pepperidge Farm, because it's simple — and stuff it into that bad boy.

5 — Season the turkey with your favorite spices; I happen to like paprika, Lawry's seasoned salt, and black pepper.

6 — Next, take a knife and poke a bunch of small holes in your turkey. You want the turkey meat to breathe in all those spices you rubbed onto it.

7 — Put it into a roasting pan, the kind with a little grill for the turkey to sit on. You don't want her sitting in the juices on the bottom.

8 — In the bottom of the pan, put 2 cups of water, four sticks of butter (sliced), salt & pepper, and whatever else you like. Put some tinfoil on the turkey and put her in the oven!

9 — Every 2 hours, open the oven and baste the turkey with those juices on the bottom, all night long, like the Lionel Ritchie song says!

10 — When you get up for the day, turn the oven temperature up to 300, but keep an eye on it. I do this because I like to eat at noon the next day, that's our tradition. I recommend it: get your guests in, have 'em eat by noon, and by 2:30 they're gone! Just be sure they leave with plenty of leftovers...

Whoopi's Yam + Marshmallow Soufflé

Yams (canned)	Almond extract	Maple syrup
Lemon juice	Vanilla	Molasses
		Marshmallows

- Preheat your oven to 300°F.

- I take a whole bunch of yams — I like canned yams best, but I drain the sugar syrup that they've been sitting in — and I put 'em in a big bowl, where I mash 'em like mashed potatoes.

- I drop in some lemon juice, and 2-3 drops of almond extract, and 2-3 drops of vanilla, which I mix in there.

(cont'd)

- Then I put a tablespoon of maple syrup and a teaspoon of molasses in the bowl, mixing that up, too.

- Now I grab a casserole dish, and I layer it like you would with a lasagna. The first layer is yams, and then I put a layer of marshmallows on top. Another layer of yams, more marshmallows. Then one more layer of each.

- I wrap that bad boy in tinfoil and now that your oven is at 300°F, the soufflé can go in for 30 minutes or until the marshmallow layers have really melted nicely.

It's a pie table!

What else do you need to know?!

If you hosted everyone, they had better make their way to the kitchen to help wash dishes!

When everyone's cleaning up together, it becomes kind of a communal thing in your kitchen, because what you've really done is

you've just fed the community.

And now the community gets to come and hang out in the kitchen where no one's been but you—so when you're cooking, feel free to mess that place up!

And unless you like leftovers for weeks, send them off with your guests!

CHRISTMAS

Growing up, it was just me, my mother, and my brother.

I had no idea we were poor, because my mother made us rich.

When I was a kid, and Christmas got close, we'd get out of bed one morning and there'd be stencils on the windows made out of window wax–it's pink and thick and looks like Pepto Bismol. So, suddenly, there were Santas and Christmas trees on the windows and we'd go, "WOW!" and my mother would go, "What?" We'd say, "You didn't see the . . .?" And she'd say, "Oh, okay. Just clean it up when you're done."

So then the next day, you'd wake up and there'd be a tree. Just a naked tree standing in the living room. "Who brought the tree?" we'd ask, but she'd say, "I don't know why you keep asking me these questions." And the next time you woke up, there'd be stuff on the tree. So this goes on and on, and each night more happens. Come Christmas Eve, our heads would be spinning: something's happening but we don't know why! We'd think, "Well, clearly we're not getting anything because there's nothing under that tree." But we had the lights and the ornaments–it was always a beautiful tree– so we were good. That night we would tiptoe out, and we'd see that my mother was in her bed.

Under the tree: nothing. So we didn't pop up Christmas morning (she knew what she was doing) but eventually my brother would come into the room like Road Runner, shouting, "Get up, get up!" And under the tree was everything that we never asked for.

Literally almost to the day she died, my mother would say, "I just don't know what you're talking about, you ask me this every year." And she'd stalk off. My mother deserved an Oscar.

———

There was not a Christmas that came where we didn't feel like we were the richest kids in the world.

———

Not because we got stuff (and we got stuff) but because this woman understood that you have to make things wonderful for children. It's your job to make stuff magical, even if you don't feel magical. I know there are a lot of people out there who did not have good family relationships, whose parents were not good for them, but there are other people around you who are. And you can make your family. You can start a tradition even if you weren't handed one, and you can make it any way you want to.

So remember how, throughout the book, I keep saying I have a lot of stuff? Well, if you thought I had a lot of stuff before, you can't imagine how much Christmas and Hanukkah stuff I have. There are reindeer, there are Santas riding on reindeer, there's so much Christmas stuff in the house —— we couldn't fit it on the table. ——

And really, your Christmas dining room table is all about the people around it.

What you do with your family, at your Christmas table, is your tradition.

For me,
it's all about Christmas day,
just because of how my brain works.
I can't do more than that.

I cook twice a year—that's it.

So if you wanted Christmas Eve, you're not getting
jack on Christmas day; pick your day.

———

A Christmas Story is on loop all day, doesn't matter where they are in
the movie, you just turn on TBS and that's all you see. You'll be doing
other things in other rooms, but you'll hear a line from the TV,
so you'll run in and shout, "Fra-gee-lay! It must be Italian!"
And then you run out until, "You'll shoot your eye out!"
So everyone's doing different things in different
places in the house, but they all come
running when they hear, "Food!"

This was made by
Mark Roberts, a designer
who's very famous for his elves and
Santas. He gave me this a few years ago.

I said, "This looks an awful lot like me!"

And he said, "No, no … no, no."
But I feel like that's a
Whoopi elf.

Christmas morning, everyone comes down and we all open presents. Then everyone goes to put things away and asks:

What time are we eating?

Everybody makes their way back and friends arrive who are coming over to be part of the madness.

And we eat and we laugh, and talk about how grateful we are to have this life.

Santa and I have a very unique relationship. Whenever I talk about Santa, I explain that he and I are friends. And that there are things that he has asked to have happen because if you're doing all that work up in the North Pole, you really can't be everywhere you need to be. And he does it himself, he doesn't take the elves. So his missive has been to several of us (since I'm actually not the only one) that they can amass what children would like to have. There are some Santas who like to make people give, which is why you see the Santas with the kettles. Sometimes Santas make children feel better—you'll see Santas in hospitals, because when kids can't be home, he likes to make sure that they know he's also thinking of them.

I've put together as many different kinds of Santas as I can find.

And because there are so many different colors in the world, you'll see lots of different color Santas. In a funny way, it's the truth of when you believe in something, wanting that thing to look like you and be part of you.

Santa's not caught often, but occasionally it has happened, and what he explained to me is that he will appear to be whoever is catching him. If they're Tibetan monks, Santa will appear to be bald (with a beard, the beard never goes) but he's in the monk garb. I've tried to put together as many different kinds of Santas as I can find. When kids come to my house, I want them to feel like their Santa is here. If you don't believe I'm friends with Santa, watch *Call Me Claus*... you'll see!

You'll note that the Johnson Brothers have lots of different styles of plates. These are some of my favorites because it's "The Night Before Christmas." I almost had the entire poem collected, but I was missing one little stanza, and for months I couldn't track it down. But someone found it for me, and it turns out, it was on the punch bowl!

P.S. Johnson Brothers, can you make it a little easier on us next time?!

Here's what I celebrate at the holidays: everything! Everything. I celebrate Hanukkah, I celebrate Christmas, I celebrate Kwanzaa...'cause why not? It's a whole bunch more fun.

This isn't a time for your best china,

which might go without saying!

I like to throw beads on the table and other fun things for people to grab, but they need to be accessible so people will actually take them.

I've always wanted to make the international Santa and
the international nativity collection, since it doesn't exist.

———

That's how Patience Brewster ended up making this Nativity. I called her and asked,
"Can you make a Nativity with maybe a black dad and a white mom and a mocha baby?
'Cause that's kind of how our family is." So she said, "Of course!" and made mine, and then
she said, "How did I not do this a long time ago?" And I said, "Well, I saw where I was not."

When I was little and Christmas got close, my mom would take us to FAO Schwarz. I love FAO because it didn't matter if you had money or not, they allowed you to bring your children to look and touch everything. Kids who had nothing could come and be part of the magic. You can touch things, you can hug things, you can dream—it's very aspirational.

By the way, FAO still lets you bring your kids in and for no money whenever you like. I bet you have holiday decorations in your town. Take an afternoon, get a couple of thermoses, fill 'em with hot chocolate and marshmallows, and go around town. *Participate, participate, participate and LIVE!!!*

I once asked my mom, "Why did you bring us to FAO when you knew we couldn't afford..." She said, "It wasn't about what we could buy; it was about what you could think about having." And she was right: I didn't need a ninety-foot giraffe, because we lived in the projects. But when they talk about sugarplums dancing in your head—that, to me, is FAO Schwarz.

Let us always be clear:

little kids do not think about holidays the
same way we do. As adults, we're told we should
be thinking about everything good for mankind,
but when you're a little kid, it's about toys.
And it should be because they'll figure out what they
have to work on when they grow up; yes, we have to
be more thoughtful; yes, we have to be kinder.
But you're allowed to be selfish when you're a kid!
You want to have a great holiday season?

*Stop trying to orchestrate it,
and just enjoy it.*

NEW YEAR'S

I never
travel on New
Year's, I stay home—
so friends come to
→ me. ←

We play charades, we bring
out all kinds of games, and we
serve lots of alcohol (which I
don't drink), along with little
sandwiches and things to
snack on. It's a potato chip
kind of night.

And with all that alcohol
flowing, I don't want anyone
driving home, so I always
keep four or five sleeping bags
nearby, and it can become a
big sleepover. We'll all go
down to the movie room
and there'll be 35 people
down there watching
Ryan Seacrest
as the ball
drops.

IF YOU LIKED IT ON MY TABLE

here's some suggestions of places where you can find it for your table…

Let me tell you something about all the stuff you see in this book:
I bought it, I found it, and I had to go looking for it—which sometimes took months or years—
but I'm eliminating some of that wear and tear on you, because I don't want you to
see something and not be able to know where I got it!
There's a lot of great stuff in here that is readily available.
Some of it, not so much, but that's the joy of
searching for treasure.

"212 Skyline" and "Intervention" table settings
made by & found at:
Fishs Eddy (fishseddy.com;
look it up—a place for great plates)

**Birdcage-themed
3-tier plate stand**
made by: Utopia by Chefline
found at: Amazon UK (amazon.co.uk)
(was not available to ship to US)
try: eBay (ebay.com)

"Good Idea" glass
made by & found at:
Highwave (highwave.com)

**High-heel shoe
wine glasses**
made by & found at:
Yurana Design
(yurana.com)

Vintage jelly/juice glass
found at: eBay (ebay.com)

Silk fall leaves
made by: Bassion
found at: Amazon
(amazon.com)

**"'Twas the Night
Before Christmas" and
"His Majesty" plates**
made by: Noble Excellence /
Johnson Brothers
found at: Replacements, Ltd.
(replacements.com)
also try: Amazon and eBay
(amazon.com and
ebay.com)

**Thanksgiving
leftover containers**
made by: Live and
Let Buy Containers
found at: Amazon
(amazon.com)

Christmas taper candles
found at: MacKenzie-Childs
(mackenzie-childs.com)

Santa doll
made by:
Santa's Workshop
found at:
The Black Art Depot
(blackartdepot.com)

**Kids' Thanksgiving activity
tablecloth**
made by: Turkey Supply Co.
found at: Amazon
(amazon.com)

Bone Appetit paper plates
made by: Talking Tables
found at: Amazon (amazon.com)

Moving flame battery-operated candles
made by: Luminara
found at: Amazon (amazon.com)

Skull mason jar with straw
made by: Studio by Godinger
found at: Amazon (amazon.com)

Knife rests
try: Amazon and eBay (amazon.com and ebay.com)

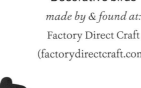

Decorative birds
made by & found at: Factory Direct Craft (factorydirectcraft.com)

Individual salt and pepper shakers
try: eBay, Etsy, Amazon, and Tiffany (ebay.com, etsy.com, amazon.com, and tiffany.com) to hunt for different kinds (I've never been able to find these rare ones again!)

Artificial spider web
made by: Amscan Inc.
found at: Party City (partycity.com)

Yellies!
made by: Hasbro
found at: Amazon (amazon.com)

Day of the Dead decor
made by: Amscan Inc.
found at: Party City (partycity.com)

THANK YOU

I would like to thank the team that helped me make this book:

Arnold Wilkerson, Danny Garcia, Joy Ganesh, and all
the Bakers at The Little Pie Company

·

D&D London / Bluebird London NYC
Jared Sexton, Executive Pastry Chef
Colby Lehman, Events Manager

·

Ellen Gordon, Tootsie Roll Industries

·

Marlo Phillips, Marlo Flowers LTD

·

Angelo Sinclair

·

Maria Rizzo

·

Nicole Leven

·

Tom Leonardis

·

Stephanie Suski

·

James Jahrsdoerfer

·

Charli Rose Burr-Reynaud

·

I would also like to thank my amazing publishing team.
(If you want to know who they are, flip the page…)

First published in the United States of America in 2019 by
Rizzoli International Publications, Inc.
300 Park Avenue South · New York, NY 10010
www.rizzoliusa.com

Developed in conjunction with Jill Cohen Associates, LLC.
Photography: Laurie Frankel
Styling: Helen Crowther

Publisher: Charles Miers
Editor: Aliza Fogelson
Creative Direction: Chip Kidd
Design: Mark Melnick
Narrative Consultant: Lucy Carson
Production Manager: Barbara Sadick
Managing Editor: Lynn Scrabis

Printed in Italy

2019 2020 2021 2022 / 10 9 8 7 6 5 4 3 2 1

ISBN: 978-0-8478-6698-4
Library of Congress Control Number: 2019938295

Visit us online:
Facebook.com/RizzoliNewYork
Twitter: @Rizzoli_Books
Instagram.com/RizzoliBooks
Pinterest.com/RizzoliBooks
Youtube.com/user/RizzoliNY
Issuu.com/Rizzoli

Thanks for coming!

*You know you had
a good time!*